Mike and Spike

Written by
Debbie Strayer

Illustrations by
Joy Majewski

New Sounds:

i_e

Common Sense Press

© 1998 by Common Sense Press

Printed 09/15

8786 Highway 21 • Melrose, FL 32666

ISBN 1-880892-59-6

Mike and Spike like to ride bikes. They ride on the side. They like to hike.

1

They will ride to the trail.
The road is not wide.

2

Yikes! Do not go down the side.

The road winds. Can they find the trail?

This man is kind. He will help the boys. They will find the trail.

5

Mike and Spike do not mind. There is the trail. The bikes will glide.

Stop the bikes! They will get on the trail. Time to hike.

The trail is wide. Mike and Spike have fun when they hike.

New Words:

i_e

Mike	wide
Spike	yikes
ride	slide
side	glide
hike	time
bikes	

stop

New Sight Words:

road   boys   down   do   there

Review Words:

the	and	on	trail	will
to	can	not	this	is
they	man	help	have	when
he	get	go	like	fun

Word Family:

-ind

find

kind

mind

winds